A Character Building Book™

Learning About Creativity from the Life of
Steven Spielberg

Erin M. Hovanec

The Rosen Publishing Group's
PowerKids Press™
New York

To my mom, Mary Ellen Hovanec
A promise kept

Published in 1999 by The Rosen Publishing Group, Inc.
29 East 21st Street, New York, NY 10010

First Edition

Book Design: Erin McKenna

Photo Credits: p. 4 © Kosta Alexander/Archive Photos; p. 7 © DOC/M.P.A./The Gamma Liaison Network; p. 8 © King/The Gamma Liaison Network; pp. 11, 20 © Archive Photos; p. 12 © Paul Lender/Corbis-Bettman; pp. 15, 19 © The Gamma Liaison Network; p. 16 © Corbis-Bettmann.

Hovanec, Erin M.
    Learning about creativity from the life of Steven Spielberg / by Erin M. Hovanec.
        p.   cm. — (A character building book)
    Includes index.
    Summary: A brief biography of the filmmaker whose creative drive has led him to make many different kinds of movies, including "Jaws," "Jurassic Park," "Raiders of the Lost Ark," and "Schindler's List."
    ISBN 0-8239-5349-1
    1. Spielberg, Steven, 1947- —Juvenile literature. 2. Motion picture producers and directors—United States—Biography—Juvenile literature. 3. Creative ability—Juvenile literature. [1. Spielberg, Steven, 1947-. 2. Motion picture producers and directors.] I. Title. II. Series.
PN1998.3.S65H68 1998
791.43'0233'092—dc21
[B]
                                            98-25693
                                              CIP
                                              AC

Manufactured in the United States of America

Contents

Growing Talent

Steven Allan Spielberg was born on December 18, 1946. While he was growing up, Steven asked his mom and dad lots of questions. He liked to know how things worked. Once he even threw a cherry pie up onto the ceiling because he wanted to see what would happen! Steven's mom and dad knew he had an active **imagination** (ih-MA-jih-NAY-shun). He loved to make up stories and to dress up in costumes. He was a very **creative** (kree-AY-tiv) boy.

◀ *Steven has become famous because of his creativity.*

A Homemade Movie

When Steven was twelve years old, he started making movies with his dad's movie camera. Soon Steven's homemade movies were better than his dad's! In seventh grade, Steven made a movie called *Fighter Squad*. His friends were the actors. As the **director** (dih-REK-ter), Steven told them what to do. He even asked the local airport if he could film scenes in one of the fighter planes that was kept there. The people at the airport said yes. So Steven and his friends filmed part of their movie inside a real plane.

In his lifetime Steven has worked on more than 50 films. ▶

First Prize

As Steven practiced, his movies got better. The next year he began making a movie called *Escape to Nowhere*. He filmed it in the Arizona desert near his home. This movie even had **special effects** (SPEH-shul uh-FEKTZ) like movies he'd seen in theaters. Steven's parents drove the cars in the movie and his three sisters helped too. The local news did a story about Steven and his movies. They thought he was very creative and **talented** (TA-len-ted). *Escape to Nowhere* was so good that it won first prize in the Canyon Films Junior Film Festival.

◀ *Over the years Steven has won many awards for his movies. In 1995 he received the American Film Institute Lifetime Achievement Award.*

His Big Break

After high school, Steven went to a **movie studio** (MOO-vee STOO-dee-oh) to get a job making movies. He did lots of different jobs for different movies and TV shows. Steven made friends with everyone he met, and learned as much as he could. Then he got his chance. The studio said Steven could direct a movie about a shark. Nobody thought the movie would do very well. But Steven used his creativity to make it very scary. The movie, called *Jaws*, opened in 1975 and was a huge **success** (suk-SESS). It made Steven famous.

Much of Jaws was filmed on a small boat in the Atlantic Ocean. This was the first movie ever to be filmed in a small boat on the real ▶ ocean, instead of in a large tank made to look like the ocean.

Indiana Jones

In 1989 Steven made an exciting **adventure** (ad-VEN-cher) movie. He called it *Raiders of the Lost Ark.* The movie was about a **hero** (HEER-oh) named Indiana Jones. So many people liked Indiana Jones that Steven made two more movies about him.

Some scenes in these movies would be hard or dangerous to film with the actors. So Steven used tiny cars with puppets in them to look like real people in real cars. This was a creative way to keep the actors safe, and it also saved Steven money.

◀ *Actor Harrison Ford has played Indiana Jones in all three movies.*

13

Dinosaurs!

In 1993 Steven decided to make a movie about dinosaurs. It was called *Jurassic Park*. He made another one in 1997 called *The Lost World*. Steven wanted the dinosaurs to be huge and to look very real in these movies. He knew he needed to use computers to make the dinosaurs look real. But he didn't know much about computers. So he learned. With the help of other people, Steven's computer dinosaurs looked like they were alive. People were **amazed** (uh-MAYZD) by these movies.

Steven likes working with creative people, such as actors Jeff Goldblum and Julianne Moore. Here ▶ they're on the set of The Lost World.

A Sad Subject

Steven liked action movies, but he wanted to make movies that would help people too. One movie, called *Schindler's List*, was about a man who saved the lives of Jewish people during World War II. It was a sad movie and Steven didn't know if people would like it. But Steven is Jewish, and this movie was important to him.

People around the world loved *Schindler's List*. It taught them important lessons about helping people. It even won two Academy Awards: for Best Director and Best Picture.

◀ *Steven learned that he could be creative when making a serious movie during the filming of* Schindler's List, *in 1993.*

Giving Back

Steven's movies have been very successful, and he's made lots of money. He uses much of that money to help people.

During World War II, people called **Nazis** (NOT-zees) stole from, hurt, and killed millions of Jewish people. Steven wants to make sure that people around the world know about this. Steven hopes that if people know about what happened, it will never happen again. Steven gives money to **museums** (myoo-ZEE-umz), TV shows, and movies that are about Jewish people and their hard times.

Teaching the world about what happened to Jews during World War II is very important to Steven. ▶

Trying Something Different

In his movies, Steven likes to do new things. He always wants to try something different. Sometimes he doesn't direct movies, but **produces** (pruh-DOO-sez) them. Some of the movies he's produced are cartoons, like *An American Tail* and *Tiny Toon Adventure*. Some are funny, such as *The Flintstones* and *Men in Black*. Others, like *Twister*, are filled with action. Steven can always **imagine** (ih-MA-jin) fun and interesting stories. He is creative and he comes up with new ideas all the time.

◄ *Producing* The Flintstones *in 1994 was a lot of fun for Steven.*

New Dreams

For many years Steven had directed movies for movie studios owned by other people. But in 1994 he decided he wanted to run his own movie studio. So he and two other men began their own studio. They call it DreamWorks. Today, DreamWorks makes movies and TV shows.

Steven is now very busy at DreamWorks. He says he will never get tired of making movies. Steven likes using his imagination every day. Telling stories in new and creative ways is what he loves best.

Glossary

adventure (ad-VEN-cher) An exciting thing to do.

amazed (uh-MAYZD) Happily surprised.

creative (kree-AY-tiv) Having good, new ideas.

director (dih-REK-ter) The person who tells the actors what to do in a movie.

hero (HEER-oh) A brave, good person.

imagination (ih-MA-jih-NAY-shun) Being able to create things in your mind.

imagine (ih-MA-jin) To create things in your mind.

movie studio (MOO-vee STOO-dee-oh) A place where movies are made.

museum (myoo-ZEE-um) A place where you can go to see historic and artistic objects.

Nazi (NOT-zee) A person who stole from, hurt, and killed many people, especially Jewish people, during World War II.

produce (pruh-DOOS) To make a movie or TV show.

special effect (SPEH-shul uh-FEKT) A part of a movie that makes scenes that are fake look real.

success (suk-SESS) When something ends in a good way.

talent (TA-lent) Being able to do something very well.

Index